SEAHORSE

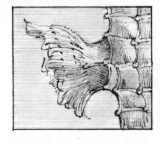

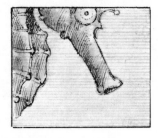

by Robert A. Morris
Pictures by Arnold Lobel

A Science I CAN READ Book

HARPER & ROW, PUBLISHERS
New York, Evanston, San Francisco, London

SEAHORSE

To my son, Everett Ashley

There is a big storm at sea.

Giant waves

break against the shore.

Many sea animals

swim to deeper water.

The water is calmer there.

But some animals

stay near the shore.

One of them is a fish.

It does not look like most other fishes.

It is a seahorse.

CRASH!

A huge wave rips the seahorse

from the seaweed.

It takes him out to sea.

He is floating free in the water.

He is in danger,

because his enemies can see him.

A small piece of seaweed floats by.

Quickly the seahorse

wraps his tail around the seaweed.

The seaweed is brown.

It is called Sargassum.

Tiny sacs are attached to its stem.

The sacs look like balloons.

They keep the seaweed afloat.

The seahorse holds tightly

to the seaweed.

The storm lasts

for days and days.

The seahorse is tired

and hungry.

He must eat soon.

If he does not eat,

he will become too weak

to hold on to the seaweed.

The storm is over.

The sea is calm.

More seaweed comes

and still more seaweed.

Soon there is a huge blanket

of brown Sargassum on the sea.

The seahorse and his seaweed

are in the middle of it.

There are many tiny animals

and plants

floating in the water.

They are called plankton.

Little fish eat plankton.

Larger fish eat the little fish.

The seahorse is very hungry.

Tiny fish swim by.

Tiny shrimp swim by.

The seahorse watches

one of the little shrimp.

It swims near him.

Suddenly the seahorse

puffs out his cheeks.

18

His mouth opens.

POOF!

19

The shrimp disappears

down his long snout.

POOF! POOF! POOF!

Three more shrimp disappear.

The seahorse does not have teeth.

He sucks in food

through his long nose.

POOF!

There goes another shrimp.

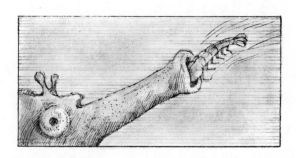

There is plenty of food

for the seahorse.

He eats hundreds of small shrimp,

until he is full.

The seahorse is brown.

So is the Sargassum.

It is hard to see the seahorse.

He looks like a piece of seaweed.

One day, a fish,

a giant amberjack, swims by.

The amberjack is hungry.

He eats small crabs and fishes.

He also eats seahorses.

The seahorse stays very still.

The amberjack swims

closer and closer.

SWISH!

He eats a small crab,

near the seahorse.

The amberjack does not see

the seahorse.

He is still hungry

and swims away

to look for more food.

One day the seahorse

lets go of the seaweed.

He starts to move

to another piece.

The seaweed is only

a few feet away.

But it is a long trip

for a seahorse.

He has nothing to hold on to.

He may be swept away.

A large fish may eat him.

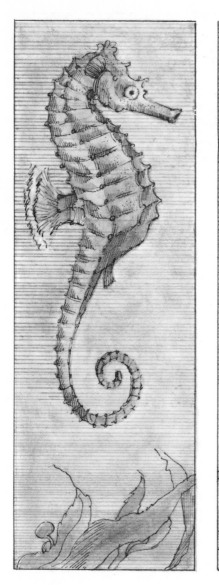

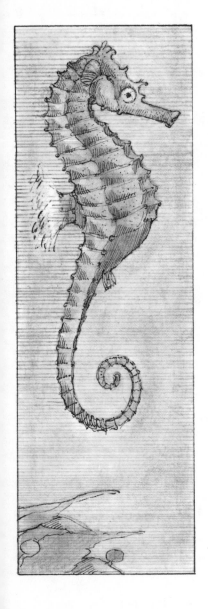

He moves
the small fin
on his back.
He moves the fin
faster and faster.
Soon it is moving
so fast that it
cannot be seen.

The fin makes

the seahorse go.

But he is swimming

in the wrong direction!

He starts moving the fins

on the side of his head.

They look like ears.

He moves one fin

faster than the other.

He quickly turns around.

The seahorse uses these fins

to turn one way or the other.

A small fin below his stomach
helps him stay up straight
in the water.
In a minute he makes the trip
to his new home in the seaweed.
He is safe now.

CLICK! CLICK! CLICK!

What a strange noise.

The underwater world is often noisy.

SNAP! SNAP! SNAP!

goes a small shrimp.

CROAK! CROAK! CROAK!

goes a fish.

Then there is *CLICK! CLICK!* again.

The seahorse has heard

this sound before.

It is the sound of another seahorse.

A seahorse makes this sound

by snapping its neck.

37

The seahorse

turns one of his eyes

to the front.

He turns his other eye

to the back.

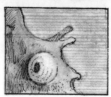

One eye moves at a time.

At last, he finds the other seahorse.

It is a female.

He swims slowly toward her

and greets her.

CLICK! CLICK! CLICK!

She is two years old.

He is the same age.

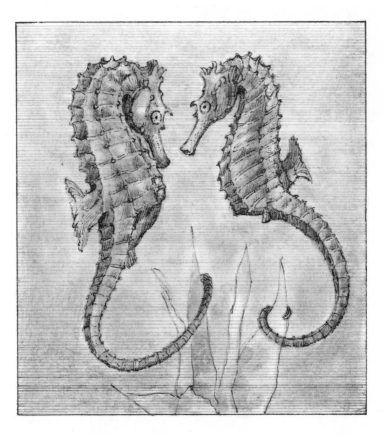

For a short time they join tails.

Then both of them

wrap their tails

around the seaweed.

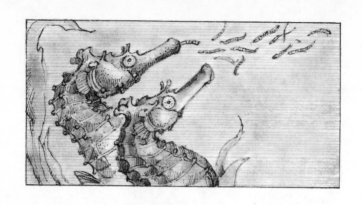

The seahorses

see many small eggs

in the water.

They are eel eggs.

When the baby eels hatch

the seahorses eat many of them.

One day the female seahorse

swims over to the male.

It is time

for the female to lay eggs.

Most fishes lay their eggs

in the water.

Seahorses do not.

The male seahorse

has a large pouch

below his stomach.

The female places the eggs

in this pouch.

The male will carry the eggs there

until they hatch.

41

Days pass and the winds blow.

The seahorses hold fast

to the seaweed.

The seaweed floats

closer and closer

to the shore.

One day the seaweed

drifts into a large bay.

The bay is calm.

It is protected

from the big waves

in the ocean.

It is a good home

for the seahorses.

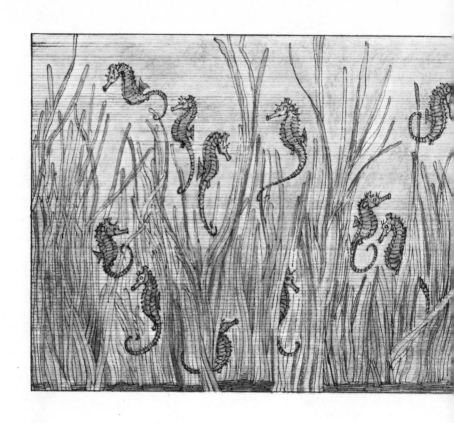

Both seahorses

swim to some eelgrass.

There are many other seahorses

living in the eelgrass.

They are black like the dark eelgrass.

It is hard to see them.

But it is easy to see

the brown male and female seahorses.

They are the same color

as the Sargassum.

A large fish called a lookdown
swims into the eelgrass.

The brown seahorses hide quickly.

The lookdown does not see them.

In two days

the seahorses have become black.

They look like the eelgrass.

Now they are safe

from bigger fish.

The male seahorse

has carried the eggs

for about twenty-five days.

His pouch is very large.

He bends over

as if he has a stomach ache.

POP!

Out shoots a baby seahorse.

POP!

Three more babies

shoot out of the pouch.

POP!

Out shoot twelve more babies.

Soon there are hundreds

of baby seahorses

in the water.

They are as long

as their father's nose.

Many of them

wrap their tails

around the eelgrass.

They start eating plankton.

They are able

to care for themselves.

Some of the babies

are carried away by the water.

They will live far from their parents.

Not all of the baby seahorses

will grow up.

Some will be eaten by larger fish.

The pouch of the male seahorse

is empty.

He looks smaller.

He will not carry eggs again

for many months.

The female stays near him.

It is nearly dark.

CLICK! CLICK! CLICK!

The seahorses in the eelgrass

are looking for food.

POOF! POOF! POOF!

The seahorses are sucking in

tiny animals.

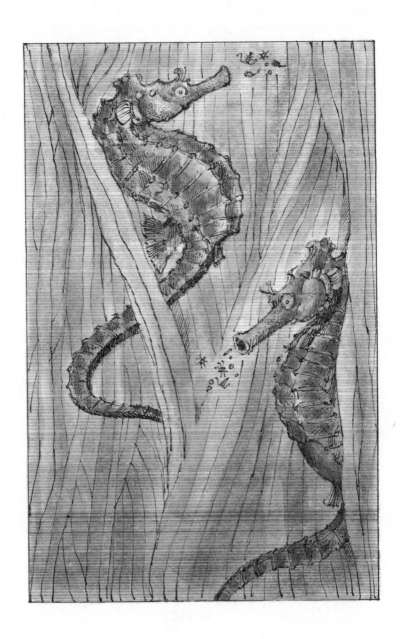

The male and female

will stay in the calm bay

for a long time.

About the Author

Robert A. Morris has been interested for many years in fishes that live in the sea. He took his Master's Degree in Marine Biology at the University of Hawaii. He was then curator at Marineland of Florida and later at the New York Aquarium. He has spent many hours watching and collecting fishes in the ocean waters around Hawaii, Florida, and the Virgin Islands.

There are many kinds of seahorses found in the oceans of the world. The seahorse in this book is found in the Atlantic Ocean.

About the Artist

Arnold Lobel has written and illustrated many I CAN READ Books, including FROG AND TOAD ARE FRIENDS, a Caldecott Honor Book.